T0208583

Old Country Wellness and Happiness Guide

TATIANA RICHARDS

BALBOA.
PRESS

A DIVISION OF HAY HOUSE

Copyright © 2019 Tatiana Richards.

All rights reserved. No part of this book may be used or reproduced by any means, graphic, electronic, or mechanical, including photocopying, recording, taping or by any information storage retrieval system without the written permission of the author except in the case of brief quotations embodied in critical articles and reviews.

Balboa Press books may be ordered through booksellers or by contacting:

Balboa Press
A Division of Hay House
1663 Liberty Drive
Bloomington, IN 47403
www.balboapress.com
1 (877) 407-4847

Because of the dynamic nature of the Internet, any web addresses or links contained in this book may have changed since publication and may no longer be valid. The views expressed in this work are solely those of the author and do not necessarily reflect the views of the publisher, and the publisher hereby disclaims any responsibility for them.

The author of this book does not dispense medical advice or prescribe the use of any technique as a form of treatment for physical, emotional, or medical problems without the advice of a physician, either directly or indirectly. The intent of the author is only to offer information of a general nature to help you in your quest for emotional and spiritual well-being. In the event you use any of the information in this book for yourself, which is your constitutional right, the author and the publisher assume no responsibility for your actions.

Any people depicted in stock imagery provided by Getty Images are models, and such images are being used for illustrative purposes only. Certain stock imagery © Getty Images.

Print information available on the last page.

ISBN: 978-1-9822-3589-5 (sc)
ISBN: 978-1-9822-3590-1 (e)

Balboa Press rev. date: 10/17/2019

Contents

Acknowledgments

I dedicate this book, and I would like to express my deepest gratitude, to my wonderful parents: my mother Eugenia and my late father Alexei, who truly represent the embodiment of the most dedicated and loving parents; my beautiful, smart and talented sister, Violeta; my awesome and witty niece, Vladi; the ever-inventing himself, Alex, without whom this book would not have existed; all my amazing and loving aunts, uncles and cousins that influenced my upbringing; all my friends, especially my friend and editor, Jen, who believed in this book more than I did and who gently pushed and inspired me to move forward; my talented editor, Rachael, who perfected my manuscript; my accountability partner, Lauren, who kept me on track and provided insightful feedback along the way; my friend, Steven-John, for a very comprehensive and thoughtful "Foreword", and to Balboa Press for publishing it! My deepest gratitude to God, Fr. Steven, Fr. Costa, Fr. Paisios, Fr. Blasko, and all the teachers over the years that built the foundation for my spiritual growth.

Editors:
Jennifer Salerno
Rachael Cave

Foreword

by Steven-John M. Harris, PhD
Licensed Psychologist
Newport Beach, California

In the 1950s and 1960s, Western culture was exploding with all kinds of medical advances and modern cures, including psychological methods. These methods were put into popular print and spread rapidly to the main public. These new "experts" seemed to offer scientific evidence that many of our assumptions about how we were living were wrong and needed correcting. This included parenting techniques that began to make even the most normal parent feel insecure or neurotic about how they were raising children. Counter to this movement, the late and great pediatrician and psychoanalyst, Donald Winnicott warned against these new-fangled methods and stressed that it was most important for mothers to trust their instincts when raising children. Abuse and parenting problems, according to Winnicott, resulted from being cut off from one's natural connection with themselves. One might imagine that one would need to go to psychotherapy to be cured of all the scientific methods that infected the mind of an otherwise healthy parent!

While not a book about parenting, it is in the spirit of returning to one's roots and traditions to cultivate healthy thoughts and habits, including diet, exercise, spiritual practice, along with other sound practices, that we graciously receive Tatiana Richards' *Old Country Wellness and Happiness Guide*. By taking us through the journey of her youth from the small Republic of Moldova under the communist rule by the USSR, and later to its crash, we learn of her life growing up in rural areas where everyone grew their own food and were not exposed to processed foods. As a cheerful and enthusiastic storyteller, we are brought on the journey of a very happy family and childhood, which later experienced financial and family losses before she migrated to the United States in her twenties. She takes us on a journey that includes responding to emotional difficulties and other health problems by the habits and healthy traditions from her background where people tend to live longer, are more active and appear to be healthier than individuals in the United States, who have become increasingly overweight and are now prone to develop more illnesses related to their overeating. Further, the American culture, while valuing youth and fitness, frequently lacks healthy activity and exercise as well as other poor health habits. By having Tatiana share her traditional knowledge about healthy habits, life learning, research and, at times wisdom, we are challenged to live better lives and to feel better.

*Further, this work is not simply a "think positive" program. The author seeks to face crises and life's difficulties head on by pointing out that **it is not our circumstances, but our minds that are pivotal in how we feel**. She steers us towards the importance of our thoughts and interpretations of our experience, rather than simply feeling bad when things only seem to be going wrong. This includes the importance of cultivating a healthy faith and spirituality.*

The author generously shares about her life and struggles and how she came to not only survive them, but also how to work steadily towards a life of health, joy and gratitude. It is hard to describe this work because it covers so much ground. Is this the guidance of a loving and nurturing friend or life-coach, a healthy and dietary guide, a guide to better emotional health, a self-help book, or the work of a spiritual guide? Happily, it seems to be kind of a combination of all of these. There are no quick fixes here. However, the material is written in a way to personalize your health improvements by setting goals, with flexibility, but with an urging to be persistent and find creative ways to integrate these healthy habits into the reader's life. While some may think the guide is for women only, many of these habits would benefit the health-seeking male.

It is with this enthusiasm that I heartily endorse this work. May the author Tatiana Richards guide you on a healthy journey!

Introduction

Presently, with the World Wide Web at our fingertips, there is a plethora of information available at every turn. Now that we have the internet, embarking on an intricate journey of self-discovery has become extremely complex, as there are way too many sources, making it challenging to choose whom to trust. Also reaching emotional and mental health is difficult when you don't know where to start. While overabundance has a habit of creating barriers in our selection and decision-making process, *Old Country Wellness and Happiness Guide* provides comprehensive and easy to utilize tools designed to help achieve a happier and healthier life. In this book, I'm prepared to lead you on this path toward a new and beautiful lifestyle by sharing how clean eating and, thinking, and toxic-free environments are the Old Country way to total-body wellness.

Just like a friend is there to help you when you fall, I am hoping this book will provide you with support and tools, and to motivate you to start looking at certain experiences in your life from a different perspective.

Likely we all know the quote, "When life hands you lemons, make lemonade." This saying always inspired me. I took that a step further, saying, "**When the lemons are bad, plant them with love and watch them blossom.**"

This simply means that we will all be dealt a bad hand at one point. It isn't an external circumstance that causes our suffering, but rather our thoughts.

There are two sides to every coin. You can choose the perspective you want to live by. By becoming aware of my thoughts, and shifting my way of thinking, I started having more control over everything that I had once perceived as negative.

In that regard, this book was designed to serve as a catalyst to encourage you to transform your life by putting one foot in front of the other toward the finish line of your personal growth.

Old Country Wellness and Happiness Guide was created from personal experiences and extensive research over many years. Over the course of this book, you will notice how simple habits, such as gratitude, for example, have the ability to produce positive results in our lives. Science shows that the practice of writing in a gratitude journal can improve sleep. And, just like the domino effect, sleep can improve your mood, leading to increased enjoyment in life—and when you enjoy life, you begin to notice there are more things for which you can be grateful. Thus, enabling the never-ending cycle of constant bliss, joy and happiness.

Some of you might be thinking, "What is a gratitude journal?" Don't worry, we'll get into that a little later, as well as ways to better yourself, ranging from self-care to your environment and diet. All of these tips and tricks have helped me reach my goals of health and wellness, which is why I created a blueprint for you to apply to your life, so you can be well on your way to a holistic life filled with joy and happiness.

My Background: A Happy Youth

"Happiness cannot be traveled to, owned, earned, worn or consumed. Happiness is the spiritual experience of living every minute with love, grace and gratitude."
Denis Waitley, Author and Speaker

Mmmm…what a blissful brand-new day! Deep breath in… and out. Stretching my arms up, I extend my body and wiggle my toes. I am bathed in a cloud of total calmness and utter satisfaction. That's how the majority of my mornings start. *True happiness, joy and love.* The feeling of pure gratitude to have the opportunity to live another day, filled with valuable lessons and exciting new opportunities. This keeps me motivated and ready to start my day.

I'll be honest, I wasn't always such an easy riser. For an extended period of time, I went through a massive depression, which affected my entire life. Don't worry, we'll get there in a few minutes. But before that, when I was a kid, it was normal for me to wake up feeling completely content. I attribute that to the tight-knit family I was raised in—the family that made me the person that I am today. To get a better idea of my childhood, I'm going to take you back to where it all started.

1

I'm originally from a tiny country in Eastern Europe called Moldova. If you've never heard of my home country, don't feel bad. Only a few people I've met here in the United States have "heard" of it stating, "Oh that's the country mentioned in *The Princess Diaries*, the movie Anne Hathaway stars in." Um…no, that's "Genovia" and it's not a real country. Moldova is a *real* country that was once part of the Soviet Union (also known as the USSR), and is known today for its wines. There were once fifteen countries in the former Soviet Union. Although each country was distinct with its own identity of languages, traditions and customs, the outside world still perceived them as one "Big Russia". I'm certain that the Communist Regime greatly contributed to the overall confusion of what the former USSR was and what was actually happening over there.

I was raised in a beautiful and serene countryside between Moldova and Ukraine where people lived rural and happy lifestyles. In my town, most of the residents raised their own animals, fruits and vegetables. Entire families would eat from their own land; they would utilize cows for milk and other farm animals for meat. Everything consumed was natural, organic and home-raised. This held true for my family as well.

My family consisted of my mother, father, sister and me. Our home was nice and quaint. Three bedrooms with warm natural light were nicely decorated by mother's great interior design style; an amazing creative quality that my sister inherited. Our house was surrounded by beautiful flower gardens, where there was an abundance of fruit trees, raspberry and black currant bushes, and various vegetables.

During the summers and school breaks, our family traveled to our grandparents in Ukraine and Moldova. With incredible fondness, I vividly remember spending one half of the summer with my mother's parents, and the other half with my father's.

One of my favorite memories is when I tried milking my grandmother's cow. Before the sun rose over the fields, I would grab my little bucket and walk down to the barn with her. It was always such a serene view and a calming feeling. Unfortunately, my attempts weren't very successful, as I didn't have the dexterity as a child, but that didn't stop me and I eventually got the hang of it. Kind of. Those memories never fail to make me smile. In fact, I still remember the sound of my grandmother's silky laugh with every one of my failed attempts. She would eventually take over, since the cow needed to be relieved and I wasn't helping much. After finishing the milking, she would pour a cup for me, my sister and our cousins. I can still remember the taste of fresh cow's milk to this day. That taste reminds me so much of my childhood. Also, raw milk from cows that graze in green pastures has incredible health benefits for our body and teeth, as described in subsequent pages.

After our morning ritual, we would follow my grandmother into the kitchen, where she would begin cooking breakfast for the family. Our meals were generally the same, with slight variations, depending on the time of year and which fruits and vegetables were in season. Cherries and strawberries were in season at the beginning of summer while plums and apples were ripe toward the end of summer. For the most part, we regularly consumed scrambled eggs or buckwheat with chicken or turkey bits, cottage cheese and sour cream. With our meal we would drink tea, either herbal or black, and usually pair that with bread and butter. And when we got tired of bread, we ate fresh polenta. Polenta is made from cornmeal, has a bread-like consistency, and pairs well with sour cream, cottage cheese, soups and stews.

My sister, my cousins, local children and I would go play in the cornfields and in the nearby forest after being done with the chores in the garden. We often played hide-and-seek, built little shacks in the corn stalks and made hair from corn silk. One time, I grabbed a pair of scissors my grandmother kept in her sewing kit and took them out in the cornfields with me trying to give haircuts to the corn stalks. And what's worse, I lost my grandmother's scissors in the cornfield that day. I was so afraid that I would get in trouble since they were grandma's only pair of scissors and the village didn't have a convenience store nearby. If she needed to go anywhere, transportation was primarily by foot and the destination would be miles away on a country road, with no asphalt on it. I never found those scissors, but my grandmother was forgiving and I didn't get into much trouble.

Up to this day I wonder how we understood each other, as local kids spoke Ukrainian and we didn't (we learned it much later), but somehow, we were able to communicate and managed to have a lot of fun! Aside from the cornfields, we would often investigate the woodlands around my grandparents' village. Our goal was to be completely immersed in nature, and our grandmother allowed us to go that far because it was absolutely safe, despite us being younger than school age. One of our greatest pleasures was to pick the wild fruits and berries that grew lavishly in the deep and hidden places of the forest where we were guided by the local children. We got really good at determining which berries were edible or not. There were all kinds of wild fruits and berries, such as wild apples, and red, yellow and black currants. Currants aren't too popular in the United States, although they contain incredible antioxidant properties, but we found them all the time in the backwoods of our grandparents' home. The forest was the perfect habitat for these bushes. They would be in perfect light, getting the morning sun, and then the afternoon shade. The woods were always a nice temperature, with constant winds, and just the right amount of humidity. If we were lucky, the berries would be growing in a patch of sunlight, which meant they would be warm from the sun, and just juicy enough that they would burst in your mouth.

Sometimes we wouldn't get back to grandmother's until late in the afternoon, but if we were lucky enough to return home in time for lunch, we would have the pleasure of enjoying her delicious borscht or chicken soup. For those of you that don't know what borscht is, it's essentially a soup made out of beets, cabbage, carrots, potatoes, onions fortified with pieces of beef and typically served with a dollop of sour cream. There are many health benefits of borscht. It aids in reducing your blood pressure and also provides liver, heart and stomach protection. Alongside the soup, grandma prepared a freshly made salad from vegetables she would pick from her garden. The base was usually tomatoes, cucumbers, bell peppers, onions and dill with either an oil dressing or a dill and sour cream dressing. Another fond memory from my childhood is of my grandfather giving the kids rides to the fields in his one-horse carriage. I never realized how smart horses were until I had the opportunity to take the reins myself sitting on my grandfather's lap. I was fascinated to see how the horses knew where to go based on the way the reins were pulled. Since we were so young, and the men typically handled the more physical labor, our daily duties would include pulling weeds, picking fruits and vegetables, and toward the end of summer, we helped harvest potatoes, carrots and other vegetables that were ripe for the fall season. We also picked grapes that my grandparents would turn into wine. Our grandmother always incentivized us when picking grapes saying: "One dress for a grape" meaning, "You pick a grape, I'll buy you a dress." I had plenty of dresses by the end of the grape-picking season.

Although all of the duties were strenuous, the most grueling task was removing bugs from our potato plants. They're called Colorado potato beetles, the major pest of potato crops and, since our family didn't spray with pesticides, they were an inevitable occurrence. It would often take hours to pick them off since our gardens were so large. You see, a regular summer day in an Eastern European country, such as Moldova or Ukraine, was extremely different from what is normal in the United States. Since growing food on our land was usual in most cases, children were expected to service the land alongside their families. Even at a young age, before we understood the necessity of work, we were instilled with love and pride for our hard work.

After a long day on the farm, we would all head in for dinner. Grandma would have prepared a well-rounded meal for us. The protein often consisted of white meat or fish, and was served with a starch of either fried or mashed potatoes. That was often served with vegetable salad as well. And for dessert, we would wind down with a cup of tea and a slice of freshly baked pastry. It was always different: sour cherry, apple, plum or cheese pastry, depending on the month and what was available at the time. We always ate the fruits and vegetables in season.

As you can see, our diet was rich with whole foods, grains and full-fat dairy, but it was a rarity for anyone to be overweight or unhealthy. You can see this in the photos below that show me at the age of three, my sister at the age of five and my aunt in her twenties, as well as the photo of me at the age of eight. I attribute this healthy characteristic to the overall lifestyle. We kept busy, either working in the gardens, or exploring the world around us. That was the case for most of the people that lived in those areas. My mother carried that diet on for us when we arrived home after the summer. Although we didn't have nearly as big a garden as my grandparents, she always provided healthy, whole-food meals for us.

When Life Hands You Lemons…

We were a regular middle-class family, as the doctrine of the Communist Regime ensured that we all stayed equal and everyone had to be the same. People would retire at the same job they started after they finished their studies. My family was slightly better off financially, as my father was earning great money due to his engineering degree and our grandparents contributed financially to our upbringing. Regardless of their circumstances, my parents always remained happy. That was actually something that I always admired in my parents. Being raised in that kind of environment contributed to my overall happy-go-lucky personality. Above all, I was raised to be a good person. I was brought up to value human beings, regardless of their economic status. Both my mother and father helped many lower income individuals. My mother often provided emotional support to young women that were raised in orphanages.

Although there was incredible harmony in our house, at times my parents weren't happy with each other. They never argued, but we could sense some tension in the air. Later we learned that my father had high blood pressure and my mom couldn't convince him to quit smoking, which was an intrinsic factor to his death of a stroke. That's when our cozy household of four turned into a household of three. I was only thirteen years old. This was a huge shock to our family. The man that used to sing songs to me and my sister, the one who taught us how to dance, loved reading books, could make anyone laugh with his smart jokes, and was incredibly intelligent and witty had passed away so young. Of course, I felt a sense of confusion. Why was this happening? Why would my hero be taken away from me? We do not know the answer to this type of questions. Although one thing I know for sure, it was a contributing factor to my spiritual awakening.

Before this, I hadn't had much of an introduction to God or religion. I was raised in an atheist home. Religion wasn't a conversation topic, as the Communist Regime was teaching us that religion is opium for the people and only uneducated people believe in God. Talk about indoctrination. At my father's passing, I heard people saying that he is in a better place, where there is no pain or sorrow, just life everlasting, and I *will* see him again when the time is right. While I didn't truly understand what that meant until years later when I discovered God, those statements gave me emotional peace.

Growing up without my father helped me develop a sense of responsibility and maturity. Knowing that he's watching over me gives me strength every single day. I learned how to rely on myself, and only myself, and not to expect someone else to care for me as much as I care for myself. Yes, all of these qualities could have been learned without losing a loved one, but who am I to question God? He has His own reasons that are not revealed to us. *Everything happens for a reason.* I truly believe that. Just like there's a reason you're here, reading this book. It's up to us to learn from our experiences and apply that knowledge to our lives and make the best out of it.

I was eighteen years old, and just finished my first year of college, when the Soviet Union collapsed. The dissolution of the Soviet Union affected my family greatly. My parents' life savings were lost in a matter of days. It was discovered that their money was considered "funny money" and was deemed completely useless. At that point, with the fear of her assets being worthless, my mother decided to buy jewelry. Inflation was getting worse every day, but she knew that purchasing something tangible like jewelry would be a smart investment in the long run. She used every last ruble (Soviet Union currency), and was only able to purchase a few simple silver rings, which she gave to me and my sister as keepsakes. Today, they are my most cherished possessions. They never fail to serve as a reminder of how fragile life can be.

…Make Lemonade

Right after college, I got a job at the State University and at the Institute of Physical Education. A few months later I was offered a job at the Presidency of the Republic of Moldova. I am proud to have worked for the first President of the Republic of Moldova, Mircea Snegur. I even have a Letter of Reference from him. Maybe one day I will put it up for auction for eBay. Any takers? It was an exciting experience for a fresh college graduate to see all of the dignitaries visiting the Presidency. Although I was twenty-two, wearing a suit and trying to portray myself as a serious person, it was the most difficult feat, as I was still very childish.

I worked in the Protocol department and one of my more regular responsibilities was to greet certain guests visiting the Presidency. It must have been after lunch, I washed my hands and noticed that there weren't any paper towels available. Rather than run to the closest washroom to grab a towel, I decided to waive my hands around as a music conductor would do, so they would dry naturally. While exiting into the lobby, I noticed that one of the guests I was to greet had arrived early. I quickly rushed over, still practicing my greeting in my head. Before this, I tended to stumble over my words, as my mouth often couldn't keep up with my thoughts. I prepared to execute the best introduction anyone would have ever heard, and upon greeting him, I completely forgot that my hands were dripping wet. We shook hands and I will never forget the look on that man's face. I could tell immediately that he'd never had an experience this level of peculiarity before. And I learned two things that day: one, I'll never make it as a conductor, and two, always dry your hands because you never know whose hand you're going to have to shake.

I attribute my success at the Presidency to my parents. They truly raised me into a strong-willed, intelligent and brave young woman. Because of them, I was lucky to have an amazing time while working for the President. I'm still good friends with a former member of the House of Commons of the United Kingdom, whom I met during that time. Unfortunately, the President lost the next election and the staff was forced to resign. It was a hard punch from life and a disappointment because I truly enjoyed my work, but I didn't dwell on it for a long time. Like I said, my parents raised me strong. I knew that this was meant to pose as a stepping-stone to something greater.

If I didn't lose my job, I wouldn't have had all the amazing opportunities that came after. I wouldn't have had the chance to work as an intern at the French Alliance, where I would later be introduced to British American Tobacco, a place that would set the foundation for my corporate acumen. That prepared me for my job at Grey Advertising, the first American advertising agency in Moldova. There, I worked as a professional in advertising and became one of the most well-paid executives in my group of friends, with the most exciting career someone could ever imagine. I worked on TV and radio commercials, promotions, sweepstakes, concerts, interacted with amazing business people from France, Germany, the United Kingdom and Romania. I had a rush of adrenalin on a daily basis due to the varied responsibilities of managing my international clients. Being a successful business-minded person led me to meet my future American husband, who was exploring various options of initiating adoption process of Moldovan children to the United States. As we both fell crazily in love with each other at first sight, he later brought me to America. My experiences have led me to firmly believe that what happened to me was the best possible thing that could have happened. And that is where a very new and different chapter of my life started!

When the lemons are bad...

I never believed I would have a culture shock upon my arrival to the United States, as I thought of myself to be a very cosmopolitan woman. I went to study abroad at the University of Sibiu in Romania, and although a neighboring country, it was still completely different from a cultural standpoint. Many lecturers that taught at the University of Sibiu were from the United States. I got along with them very well. Kimberly, my first American lecturer, patiently taught me English by reading Bible verses when I didn't speak a word of English. Somehow, one day I truly started understanding what I was reading. Kimberly's warm and big heart made me fall in love with American people and totally forget the propaganda that the Soviet Union spread about Americans over the years. All the Americans I was surrounded by were kind, professional, dedicated and confident people. Due to all of these attributes, and more, I thought when moving to the United States, that everyone else would be exactly like the American men and women I had the pleasure to meet and work with. I thought I knew it all when I came here. Boy, oh boy, was I wrong!

A short period of time after the move, I started having uneasy feelings. Everything was so different from what I'd expected it to be. Aside from the obvious, that America was far more industrialized than I could have ever imagined, the people weren't exactly what I'd pictured either. Regardless of the beautiful places my husband took me to, I couldn't help but feel an overwhelming sadness, an emotional deterioration. Although this was supposed to be a dream come true, as we were becoming successful, and we had everything we needed, I just wasn't happy. I began thinking there was something wrong with me. I had always thought of myself to be a happy person, an optimistic, "glass half full" kind of girl. I was generally the friend that everyone else would turn to because I "had my life together." And I did, for the most part, which really made me question what was happening to me. But I quickly noticed my old habits being affected by the move. I wanted to stay inside my dark bedroom and never leave, and I started putting on a considerable amount of weight. At first, I was confused about these physical and emotional changes. My habits hadn't changed that drastically. I still ate relatively well. I still got up and went to work every day. What could be happening to me?

After taking a step back and assessing my situation, I quickly realized that the culture shock of immigrating to a different county really did affect me.

I was slim up into my late twenties, as you can see in the photos, which were taken a few months prior to my relocation to the United States. I could eat anything I wanted and I wouldn't gain any weight. That changed when I came to the United States. I started gaining weight right away— thirty pounds in three months! I didn't know what was happening to me. I didn't change any of my eating habits by much, aside from larger portions of meats, and yet I was ballooning. The changes to my diet didn't strike me as odd at first, but then I began to realize the culprit of my weight gain wasn't attributed to the amount of food I was eating, but rather the quality of food that I was consuming.

One of the first things I noticed upon moving to this country was that the food was completely different from what I was used to in Moldova. Not only did I learn that people go to grocery stores for the majority of their food, the food itself wasn't of the same quality that it was back home. Years ago, my best friend left for a trip to Ireland for thirty days. After leaving for her trip, she remembered she had left bread on top of her refrigerator and I remember joking that it would be covered in mold by the time she returned. But, to our surprise, the bread was perfectly fine. If anything, it looked fresh, as if she'd just returned with it from the market. I was in awe. This was completely appalling to me since bread in my native country would get moldy within three days. I was equally sickened by learning that the milk didn't spoil after three days like it did back in Moldova.

This was the first spark that got me curious about what kind of food I was ingesting in America. As life happened, the dark clouds of depression absorbed me. I was crying inside the house for days, unable to drag myself outside for a walk on the beach, which was one of my favorite past times. Nothing really seemed to bring me joy and that state of mind lasted for what felt like an eternity. Even during my weight gain, I didn't put two and two together. Only much later did I discover that there was a connection between the food that I was eating and my inactivity to my weight gain and depression.

So why am I sharing all of this with you? Because, with all of the adversities I've faced in my life, it finally occurred to me that my experiences could be beneficial to other people. Throughout the years, I have shared tips and tricks about health and wellness with friends, and they wanted to learn more. My old-world practices and discoveries, which are common knowledge to me, are specialized information to others.

Several friends of mine have recommended that I start sharing my advice on either a blog or a website. After hearing this suggestion for some time, and giving it a lot of thought, this book came about! I have always wanted to do more. Even if I can help only one person, it would make me very happy to know that I am contributing to this world in a positive way.

... Plant Them With Love...

Eventually, I was fed up. I needed to do something to get myself out of this depression. Instead of feeling sorry for myself, I decided to act. The first advance was sharing my symptoms with my doctor. I told her how I felt like I was stuck in a dark haze and I didn't know which way was up or down anymore. I had no ambition. I had no drive. I had no happiness. I left the doctor's office with a prescription for Zoloft, that I have never filled. I was somewhat familiar with Zoloft from seeing ads on TV and I recalled that Zoloft corrects the imbalance between Nerve A and Nerve B in the brain, thus alleviating the symptoms of depression. As my brain is my most precious asset, I was immediately hesitant about taking it. I believe that there are situations where antidepressants can be useful, and can even save lives, but taking medication was something that I was completely reluctant to do. I also deeply believe, and have proven in my own life, that many of the symptoms of depression can be overcome with natural measures and a little intention.

I asked my doctor if there were any other alternatives and she stated, "Sure, you can go for a walk every day for thirty minutes and you will get the same results." What? Did I hear that correctly? My doctor stated that walking for *thirty minutes a day* could give the *same result* as taking *prescription medication*? And if you couldn't guess it by now, upon finding this out, I was furious. If I didn't know any better, by now I would probably be addicted to these legal drugs. I could just imagine doctors rampantly prescribing Zoloft all around the country.

When I got home from my doctor that day, I did a thorough investigation on Zoloft. At that time, I came across information that talked about incentives for doctors who prescribe these types of medications. Sometime after that I spoke to a friend of mine, who was an executive at a very well-known pharmaceutical company. She admitted that every doctor records all the prescriptions he or she prescribes in a database, so, at the end of the quarter, the pharmaceutical company knows exactly how many prescriptions each doctor wrote. The top performers are rewarded by being invited to so-called "trainings" that take place at the most luxurious resorts in the world. While at these trainings, doctors are required to attend at least one seminar, but after that they can do whatever they please and the entire trip is paid for by the pharmaceutical company. It is quite an incentive. Pharmaceutical companies cannot directly pay doctors for prescribing their drugs, so they have become creative about the ways in which to incentivize doctors to prescribe their drugs to patients. That may be why my doctor was quick to suggest Zoloft instead of telling me to get my butt off the couch and get active for thirty minutes a day.

During my research I came across studies that show the importance of positive affirmations and a funny story popped into my head. When I was in college, a few friends of mine were talking about one of their roommates. For the sake of the story, let's call him Bill. Every morning, Bill would repeat positive affirmations to himself in the mirror. Of course, to a few immature college students, they thought he was weird and often made fun of him. But to their surprise, he was passing all of his classes with straight "As", while the jokesters were barely scraping by. This was the first time that I realized how powerful words can be when we speak them positively to ourselves.

Brain scans show that our brain lights up like a Christmas tree when we point out our best characteristics and tell them to ourselves. Constructive declarations can actually influence the chemical composition of blood cells and brain cells. Look at it like a placebo effect. When one group is given a real pill and the other is given a placebo, such as a sugar pill, they can, in many cases, yield the same results. That's because our brain doesn't know the difference between what's real and what's not real. And further, our brain acts on belief. Since that's the case, I'd rather feed my brain positive thoughts so it would manifest those beliefs outward. But that's not what I was doing. I was tearing myself down, not building myself up.

Then I got to the point where I tried anything to get out of depression. I joined a gym and started walking for twenty to thirty minutes every day. While exercising, I could feel on top of the world—and then, a few hours later, the dark clouds of depression would consume me again. So, I reasoned that physical activity was not the total solution to my problem. I continued researching. And then I discovered how I feel about myself is just as important as my physical health. The ground zero of an improved life begins in the mind. I uncovered that what I believed, that my sadness was a result of my circumstances, was the exact opposite of the truth. The reality of life is that our circumstances are the result of our thinking, not the other way around. I didn't like myself. I didn't like my body. I was tearing myself apart in my head because I didn't have the perfect life that I expected. It wasn't until much later that I learned that I needed to accept, love, appreciate, forgive and respect myself. It was hard because my mind was clouded. I could only see the most "awful" (in my perception) aspects of myself and my life. If something positive happened to me to make me think otherwise, I would negate it with a thought about a situation that would prove that I was miserable. I was a constant emotional yo-yo.

Then it hit me...I needed to get back to my roots and analyze my ancestors' eating, thinking and behavioral patterns. I originally thought of my grandparents and their long lives. My grandfather died at the age of eighty-three from pneumonia. He was a World War II veteran, so it's not like he had an easy life. Up until his last moments, his brain was highly functioning, and he was lucid, fully aware of his surroundings and current political events, and could have a conversation on any topic. When I was in college, he wrote me frequently. His letters were coherent, intelligent and very informative. No typos either! My grandmother lived until ninety-three and she had epilepsy for more than fifty years. That was a miracle in itself, as her neurologist warned that people with epilepsy have a much shorter life span. She had a long and productive life.

As mentioned earlier, everyone around me growing up was very active, spending most of their time doing strenuous physical labor, and rarely kicked their feet up. For fun, they attended gatherings where a lot of dancing, socializing and relaxing were taking place. Everyone I grew up around was optimistic and took everything lightly. As for the food, the meals were characterized by well-rounded nutrition including protein, vegetables, starch and dairy.

That got me thinking about the differences in European and American cultures. By comparing my lifestyle in Europe to my lifestyle here, I realized that I have been eating larger portions and haven't been as active as I should be. And the answer to my problems was to reverse the lifestyle I've adapted since moving to the United States. That's when I realized that I needed a mind hack. I needed to rewire my brain in order to resurrect like a Phoenix from the ashes.

…and Watch Them Blossom

To make it easier to focus on the best aspects of my life, I started a gratitude journal. A gratitude journal is essentially a culmination of positivity. A diary written to oneself of everything for which they are grateful. The intention is to focus on the beneficial aspects of our lives, to appreciate what we have and to remember that we should be thankful. As Brené Brown, PhD, LMSW states: *"[I] never talk about gratitude and joy separately, for this reason. In twelve years, I've never interviewed a single person who would describe their lives as joyful, who would describe themselves as joyous, who was not actively practicing gratitude."* Just think about this. You wake up, stub your toe, get into the shower and realize you ran out of shampoo; on your way to work, you get a flat tire on the freeway. Misery loves company. Now you're officially in a horrible mood. This is when you have to change your thinking. Take a deep breath and start focusing on gratitude. You hit your toe, and it's throbbing in pain, but at least you have a toe. You ran out of shampoo? Big deal! At least you have a shower and hot water, which is a *luxury* in many third-world countries. And so, what if your car's tire popped? Be grateful that you have a means of transportation.

And just like that, you'll start seeing the improvement right away. You just went to Starbucks and the person in front of you bought you your favorite drink, at Costco another cashier opens and you are invited to move to that line, you're twelve cents short at the store and the cashier says, "Don't worry, I got it." You get the picture?

I started with a gratitude journal and wrote in it every day, morning and night. I wrote down everything that I could think of to be grateful for, such as the roof over my head, running water, the blanket on my bed, the food on my table, my family that loves me, my cat that follows me everywhere I go, the blue sky, my car that takes me to beautiful places, the roads I drive on without any potholes, *anything* that would put me in a state of gratitude. And I immediately noticed a change. I started to feel that spark that I once had as a kid. The feeling of the girl that lost the scissors in the corn fields, the girl that rode on her grandfather's lap in his horse drawn carriage, the girl that danced on her father's toes and listened to him sing her to sleep. She was starting to come back to me.

You don't have to allow circumstances to dictate your mood, because the secret is that your mood dictates your circumstances. Let that sink in for a moment.

Upon changing my habits, I quickly realized I wasn't aware of the nutritional elements of processed foods and what they do to our bodies. In Moldova, the food was whole and fresh, straight from the garden, actual food. I had no idea that the products I was buying here weren't actual food, but rather "food-like." Occasionally I would eat canned foods, such as canned tuna, soup and even spaghetti sauce from a jar with my pasta. But while doing my research, I realized that even a small, seemingly insignificant portion of processed food can wreak havoc on your body. Not only can they imbalance your hormones, but they can affect your liver to the point that it can't effectively perform because of all the salts, preservatives and chemicals the food industry adds to processed foods.

I thought back to my grandparents, and their grandparents before them, who drank full-fat milk every day until the day they passed away. I thought it would be a great idea to start drinking milk, too, but I realized that even organic milk can be inflammatory if it's pasteurized. The enzymes that are beneficial to our body get destroyed in the pasteurization process, and my body couldn't tolerate it. (As raw cow milk is easily processed by our body and is incredibly beneficial to our teeth, I have reintroduced raw milk into my diet and I don't have any of the lactose intolerance symptoms I would experience drinking pasteurized organic milk. Raw milk can potentially carry harmful bacteria, therefore, please consult your doctor before introducing it into your diet.)

I took to the cupboards and threw away anything that wasn't cooked fresh and discarded everything that was considered a processed food. That meant giving up my favorite ice cream (one habit that had a lot to do with my inability to lose weight) and changing my eating habits so I was eating healthy foods again. The reason I discarded everything is because I knew I didn't have the willpower to have only a scoop of ice cream. If I had it in the fridge, the entire container would be gone in a matter of days. If I bought a candy bar, in moments, it would be history. My desire to be healthy was still strong, so I doubled-down on my focus and eliminated all sugars and flour from my diet. I stopped buying all the food that I knew wasn't good for me. When I eliminated sugar from my diet, my first concern was how could I drink my morning coffee? The thought of drinking coffee without sugar sounded dreadful. But the truth is, I had never even tried it before, so how could I know for sure? I started adding organic coconut oil, a bit of cinnamon and a little nutmeg. You know what? My morning coffee is absolutely scrumptious without the harmful, addicting simple sugars.

To my surprise, my taste buds changed. As I stopped eating certain foods, the cravings for them went away. It was hard at first, but I realized that, if I didn't have that type of food at home, little by little, I would forget about it—and even ignore it at the store. I coupled this practice with focusing my mind intently on the desire to feel happy and healthy.

As my quest persevered, I came upon a lot of studies regarding the usefulness of apple cider vinegar. I will tell you more about its incredible benefits in a few minutes, but this piqued my interest because my mom made it at home when I was growing up and we consumed it frequently, so it was very familiar to me. I started adding apple cider vinegar to my foods. I integrated a drink made with apple cider vinegar and warm water into my morning ritual. From early adulthood I had been suffering from gastrointestinal problems, but without much awareness. Since I began drinking apple cider vinegar regularly I feel much better. Remember the movie "My Big Fat Greek Wedding" and the Windex reference in that movie? Well, apple cider vinegar is the same to me as the Windex in that movie. I use it ALL the time on EVERYTHING…and it WORKS!

Making change is always hard. As humans, we become complacent, relying on default habits. If I was able to make these changes, I know you can, too. If you implement everything as described in the pages that follow, you will experience a transformation. I wish I could just magically use a wand and make the change immediately, but that's the same as wanting to run a marathon in a blink of the eye. Change takes time, but it's well worth it. If I was able to make the switch quickly, and achieve peace and joy regardless of negative incidents happening around me, I know you will be able to make that change. Everything in life is a learning experience. It's up to us how we apply that knowledge and what we choose to believe navigating through life.

As I share this, my uncle Frank, who survived a Nazi concentration camp, comes to mind. He survived because he didn't allow his circumstances to dictate his outcome. Rather than letting himself fall into depression, he focused on getting out of the Nazi camp alive. And he did! In Viktor Frankl's book *Man's Search for Meaning*, just like my uncle Frank, Dr. Frankl was a prisoner in a Nazi camp. His parents, his brother and his wife died in the camp. Dr. Frankl showcases the difference between those who focused on survival and those who gave in to their circumstances. The ones that survived found a meaning to their circumstance and focused on the greater purpose, which kept them alive. By changing our focus, we can actually change our experience if we so desire.

Powerful Life Hacks

Based on my life's experiences and learnings, I believe the steps below will benefit you greatly in finding inner peace, joy and happiness. Diet and exercise will not help you if you don't change the way you look at yourself. The importance of self-perception is crucial. The transformation starts from within.

Science shows that, with the right process and tools, we can change the neurological wiring in our brain, which leads to successful change. I started noticing results only when I accepted myself the way I was. God forgave me, and it was time that I needed to forgive myself for all the ways I've failed myself or others. We are humans, we make mistakes. That's the price to pay for being alive.

1. **Pray daily.** Multiple times throughout the day. Pray for your **loved** ones, your **friends**, your **enemies** and the **departed**. Give thanks for what you have. Appreciate everything and everyone in your life, even your **enemies,** as they serve as a stepping-stone to your greatness.

2. **Forgive yourself.** We all make mistakes. That's inevitable. We have to let go and move on, but I truly get it...forgiving oneself can be very challenging at times, as we are typically our own worst critics. You can start to change those negative internal thoughts by repeating positive affirmations to yourself multiple times a day, such as "I am **willing** to forgive myself" or state and focus on one positive aspect about yourself. As the path of forgiveness could be very daunting, this declaration has the ability to put the process of forgiveness in motion and, over time, you will think more positively and truly forgive yourself. It can take a lot of time, but trust me, it's time well spent.

3. **Forgive others.** Betrayal and negative actions are inevitable in life. But, the resentment we carry is similar to ingesting poison expecting the rat to die. When you resent someone you harm only yourself, and that destructive feeling is deteriorating your mental, emotional and physical wellbeing. Sending blessings daily, praying for the ones that harmed you, and focusing on one positive aspect of that person changes the way you view the situation and how you feel about it. Every horrible person has something positive to offer. If someone you trust stabs you in the back, focus on the fact that she or he might do good somewhere, such as feeding the homeless, donating to charities or even offering you chocolate when you are working late. Over time we will achieve forgiveness.

4. **Accept yourself and others.** We were all created in the image of God. His work is perfect. Which means we are perfect. Remember that, no matter what you look like, however you sound, *you are perfect.* And don't forget to love thy neighbor as thyself, which means we are to love ourselves, so we can be capable enough to love our neighbor. When we put ourselves down, or criticize ourselves untruthfully, it's as if we are criticizing God's creation. We always have to remember that God loves and will *always* love us no matter what. We are perfect in our imperfections. A crooked piece of driftwood found on a beach becomes an act of beauty in the hands of a talented and persistent artist.

5. **Embrace resilience.** Last year I saw something very fascinating in my backyard. Through a tiny fissure in a tile on my patio, a little plant was growing, trying to survive. I kept an eye on it; every day, I was astonished that it beat the odds and lived another day. As time went by, and it continued to grow, I realized it was a tomato plant. Later it blossomed and I noticed a small fruit emerge from one of the branches. The plant grew to about ten to fifteen inches tall at its peak. One day I saw it lying on the ground, either knocked over by one of my cats or because the stem became too thick for the root it was holding onto. The most fascinating thing was, against all odds of nature, it was still trying to thrive and actually bear fruit in such an unnatural environment. If a tiny plant has the determination to break thought a small crack in concrete, shouldn't we, as human beings, be just as willing to bounce back, regardless of what life throws at us? We have all the tools at our fingertips, but it's up to us to use them.

6. **Keep the faith.** Although I grew up in an atheist society, I always felt there was a Higher Power and instinctively was drawn to it. I believe my parents instilled me with a good set of morals. While it took me a while to embrace God's existence, I've realized that He has been always taking care of me. No matter what, I have to keep the faith, as **everything** is possible with God. Many times, my belief in God was tested, but a huge turning point for me was

a few years ago. I was visiting my sister in Europe. I was in horrible emotional turmoil, pretending to be cheerful and smiling, since I didn't want my sister to be affected by my depression. One day, as we decided to leave the house, she and I got into the elevator in her apartment building. A lady hopped in on the way down, and out of nowhere, she turned to me, looking straight into my eyes, and said, "God wanted me to tell you that He sees your pain and He hears you." I was in total shock. This woman was a complete stranger. Neither I nor my sister had seen this lady before. How would she have any way of knowing about my emotional trouble? The woman exited the elevator before me and my sister, and, when I turned the corner to take another look at her, she was gone—as if she vanished into thin air. That was great validation that God always has my back.

7. **Start a gratitude journal.** To achieve your goals, you have to be in a positive state of mind. In order to reach that, you have to shift your conscious mind to a state of love, joy, peace and gratitude. The best way to get started on this very important internal work is to start a gratitude journal. Find ten to fifteen things to be grateful for every morning and every evening. When writing in your gratitude journal, feel what you write, don't look at it as a chore. Believe in what you're writing. Get into the emotion of your words. Research shows that gratitude boosts the neurotransmitter dopamine, which is the brain's pleasure and reward system. Also, another powerful effect of gratitude is its ability to boost serotonin. Serotonin is also known as the "happy substance," which contributes to natural happiness. This means it regulates our moods and social behaviors. Trying to identify moments you are grateful for forces you to focus on the positive attributes of your life. Trust me, there are plenty of those moments if you look for them. The more you focus on the things you are grateful for, the more positive your outlook becomes, thus training your brain to find more positive things in your life. Be truly grateful and appreciative to God for what you have.

8. **Stay in a state of joy, peace, love and harmony.** Do this every day by reading or watching a funny story. Science shows that when a person laughs for at least a few minutes, the blood cells have the ability to heal themselves, which makes the immune system improve and also puts you in a great state of mind. Identify something that resonates with you personally, that always makes you smile. I love watching kitty videos. Whenever I need a quick fix, I turn to those or think of the smiley face of my adorable niece. And these techniques never fail to bring back my peaceful state of mind.

9. **Recite positive affirmations.** Find positive declarations that resonate with you. I use affirmations that lift me up, such as *"I am perfect health. I am joy. I am peace. Everything always works out for me. Embrace change, don't resist it".* Place your affirmations by your mirror so you could start your day with a positive outlook until it gets engrained in your subconscious mind and becomes a habit you can't live without.

10. **Celebrate the good and the bad.** All the **challenges** that come your way provide valuable lessons. Embrace them and extrapolate the meaning. Every challenge contributes to your expansion and growth.

11. **Focus on the positive in your life.** Look for the silver lining in everything! There is one! A few years ago, while driving in the rain, my car lost control and it span around, hitting the middle divider of the freeway with the front and rear, and then stopped facing oncoming traffic. Scary? You bet! What's the silver lining? I've learned that after my car finished doing its pirouettes, and it came to a complete stop facing oncoming traffic, the other cars were able to stop without hitting me. And in addition I got brand-new front and rear bumpers, and a paint job!

12. **Notice the thoughts you are entertaining.** Every time a judgmental or negative thought comes your way, counter it with

two positive thoughts, so you could shift your negative thinking. Don't dwell on the negative. It's impossible to control all your thoughts. No one is attempting to do that, just pay more attention as it's more productive to focus on the positive. While change can be challenging, we have to accept it, as it will benefit us in the long run. One technique I frequently use is saying *STOP* whenever I realize I am giving too much attention to a negative thought. That prevents me from falling deeper into the negative whirlpool.

If you truly desire a positive outcome in your life, pray, laugh, write in your gratitude journal, become more active, recite your affirmations and shifts into the right direction will start happening.

Creative Ways to Become More Active

*W*e all are pressed for time. As cliché as it sounds, time is fleeting. I often find myself questioning if there are enough hours in a day. For me, I find it quite challenging to find time to work out. And because of that, I had to become creative by learning to incorporate exercise into my daily routine. While I'm waiting for my eggs to boil in the morning I do variations of twenty squats, twelve push-ups against the kitchen counter, as it's easier, or twenty jumping jacks. Also, while brushing my teeth in the morning, I try to incorporate similar activities, such as walking in place and doing squats.

Another easy workout to implement into your daily routine is to take the stairs at work, park your car a bit further everywhere you go so you have a nice little walk to your destination. Walk to your colleague's office instead of calling or emailing him or her. Just go and say "Hi" to another colleague that sits on the other side of the building, or take fifteen to twenty minutes of your lunch break to go for a walk. Find yourself a colleague who will be willing to join you. Use a pedometer so you can keep track of your steps. Just seeing yourself make progress will give you a mental boost and make you feel more confident in yourself through your journey to better yourself. I have discovered HasFit.com's full-body Tabata workouts and love them. They are quick workouts that are easy to fit into a busy schedule and, guess what, they're super effective. You need only a few minutes. So, by doing what I am suggesting, you can easily fit thirty minutes of physical activity into your everyday schedule. Studies show that you will get significant health results if you just move for a half hour each day.

Feeding Your Mind

"It is not the critic who counts; not the man who points out how the strong man stumbles, or where the doer of deeds could have done them better. The credit belongs to the man who is actually in the arena, whose face is marred by dust and sweat and blood; who strives valiantly; who errs, who comes short again and again, because there is no effort without error and shortcoming; but who does actually strive to do the deeds; who knows great enthusiasms, the great devotions; who spends himself in a worthy cause; who at the best knows in the end the triumph of high achievement, and who at the worst, if he fails, at least fails while daring greatly, so that his place shall never be with those cold and timid souls who neither know victory nor defeat."

– Theodore Roosevelt

Setting and Pursuing Goals

Deciding to make a change is the first step in the process of setting goals for yourself. **Making decisions** forces your brain to feel that you have total control, which reduces stress and gives you a higher chance of achieving success.

Before you start making astronomical changes to your current situation in life, it is for you to know what your goals should look like. You need to have a clear picture of what you are expecting to accomplish. It's like using a navigation system in your car, you can't tell it to take you "there," you need to enter the street name, building number and the city you are trying to reach. Otherwise, you'll be driving in circles, which is exactly what could happen with your life destination. Be as specific as possible with your goals.

Try to look at the **bigger** picture. Start with the end in mind and focus on where you're headed. See the big reason **why** it's so important for you to accomplish your goal. The inner work is a critical part of reaching your goals. Once you set the foundation for your success, you will be amazed at results you will experience with a little bit of work. Don't look at your setbacks as failures, rather as a short detour from the correct path. The well-known author of the Harry Potter series, JK Rowling, was rejected almost two dozen times when trying to publish the groundbreaking *Harry Potter and the Philosopher's Stone*. She was a single mother, living on welfare, and of the more popular rejections she heard was that she should "get a day job," as she would never make any money in children's books. But that didn't stop her, if anything, those rejections made her more determined to advance forward. As we all know, her persistence paid off. As Thomas Edison stated: "Our greatest weakness lies in giving up. The most certain way to succeed is always to try just one more time." If he decided to give up after multiple unsuccessful attempts, the invention of the light bulb would have most likely been delayed. Success takes time. Be patient and persistent!

Write down goals of what you are going to accomplish.

Get a journal and a funky pen. **Write it down**. The reason it's important to write your goals down is that our brain takes us seriously when it sees things written down. Studies have shown that writing your goals down will dramatically increase the likelihood of achieving them. Also, we are more likely to achieve our goals if we dissect them into several shorter goals—especially if you have not been very successful at achieving your goals in the past. It's more believable for our brain when we have outlined baby steps. I'll give you an example. If one of your goals is to release thirty pounds in a year (I prefer the term "release," as our brain is programmed to "find" the things we "lose"), the monthly goal should be two and a half pounds. This goal is a much easier for our brain to believe, which in turn makes it more possible.

The weight release goal also requires some planning ahead of your meals for the whole week. I know it sounds hard, but to make it easier, you have to purchase all your food items for the week at once. Prepare a few items that you can keep in the fridge and just take one with you to work. When you come from work you can warm it up, so you don't have to start indulging in unhealthy foods while the food is being prepared from scratch.

The Healing Influence of Laughter

It's a well-known fact that laughter is the best medicine. Science shows that laughter can promote stress relief and increase immune cells. It helps us forget about problems and makes us feel instantly happy. It also facilitates resistance to disease and even can help with cancer treatment. But is there any scientific evidence to back these facts up? I found quite a few very interesting facts that you could learn more here: http://www.oasisofhope.com/blog/2012/12/11/boost-your-immune-system-with-laughter/. Laughter can increase circulation, improve digestion and can even help with muscle tension. I have started implementing the "laughing therapy" into my own daily life.

Feeding Your Body

*H*opefully you know by now the importance of clean eating. All processed foods contain an excess of unhealthy ingredients, such as preservatives, artificial sweeteners, taste enhancers, etc. These non-food ingredients create a longer shelf life for processed foods, but hugely contribute to health issues. Here's an example.

A research conducted at the Children's Hospital in Boston, Massachusetts, looked into the effects of processed and unprocessed foods on mice. The results of the study determined that mice that consumed processed food had more body fat, higher levels of fat in the bloodstream and double the amount of fat in the liver than the group that ate unprocessed food. The bottom line is: everything that is not processed, and comes as close as possible from nature itself, is good for you. And the contrast is exactly the opposite. Processed foods are your enemy.

Another thing to keep in mind is that the majority of the foods we eat *has* to be organic. The reason I am saying "majority" is because there are a few instances when fruits can be non-organic. Bananas do not have to be organic because we throw away the peel. But, for your own benefit, you should eat whole, organic fruits, vegetable, grains, beans, legumes and proteins. Not only will this have incredible benefits on our body, but on our teeth as well.

When reading *Cure Tooth Decay Heal and Prevent Cavities with Nutrition* by Ramiel Nagel, I was astonished to learn that the food that we consume has a greater influence over the health of our teeth and gums than oral hygiene. After reading his book I have decided to reintroduce raw cow's milk to my diet, consume more butter that comes from grass-fed and/or pasture-raised cows, consume more fermented foods, eat more wild-caught fish and reduce the quantity of nuts that I love snacking on.

Friendly Foods

Below is a compiled list of food items that in my opinion have to be organic. Ideally, all meats and poultry must be organic and grass-fed and/or pasture-raised. In my opinion, this is more important than buying organic fruits and vegetables.

Food Items That Must Be Organic

All dairy

Eggs

Apples

Peaches

Nectarines

Strawberries

Grapes

Blueberries

Celery

Spinach

Sweet bell peppers

Cucumbers

Cherry tomatoes

Snap peas (imported)

Potatoes

Hot peppers

Kale

Lettuce

Collard greens

Corn

Green beans

Plums

Pears

Raspberries

Carrots

Winter squash

Tangerines

Food Items That Can Be Non-Organic

Avocados
Pineapples
Cabbage
Sweet peas (frozen)
Onions
Mangoes
Papayas
Kiwi
Eggplant
Grapefruit
Cantaloupe (domestic)
Cauliflower
Sweet potatoes (if you eat the skin, they must be organic)

Fish

Always buy wild-caught fish. Avoid tuna and other large fish. Although it may be wild-caught, these types of fish tend to have huge traces of mercury, which can be detrimental to our health. Buy smaller fish that have a shorter life span, such as sardines.

Bone Broth

It seems that bone broth has been talked about quite frequently over the last few years. Although it seems like a new health fad, bone broth has been consumed by many cultures around the world for quite some time now. Bone broth has incredible benefits for the body and health of numerous systems, as it is made from bones, organs, ligaments, etc. These are parts that we typically don't consume as a part of our western diet. It has been shown that bone broth has many benefits that help your body in many ways. Below are just a few of the benefits.

1. Reduces inflammation in the body, thus improving digestion, gut health and the immune system.
2. Promotes healthy bones, joints, tendons, ligaments and teeth.
3. Contains collagen that supports healthy hair, skin and nails.

It is a popular belief that chicken soup is the best remedy for a cold. The scientific reason for that is that our immune system is linked to our gut flora. As chicken soup has high collagen content, it helps reduce inflammation and cold symptoms.

Oils to Consume and Not to Consume

Upon arriving to the United States, I was very impressed by the variety of different types of oils. Growing up, we only used sunflower oil. We used it on salad dressings, and when sautéing and frying. And while I was married, my husband did most of the cooking, so I didn't pay much attention to the oils he was using. But I can say that I didn't like the taste of most of those oils. I attributed this to my being used to the sunflower oil. Later, I discovered that we were using all the wrong oils for years. So now I only keep three types of oil in my kitchen:

1. Coconut oil that I use for anything hot (frying, sautéing and in my coffee): It must be cold-pressed, virgin coconut oil.
2. Olive oil that I use in my salads (only on cold foods): I use both virgin and extra virgin, depending on the flavor I'm going for.
3. Avocado oil for frying, sautéing

I'm a fan of, and have the utmost respect for, Dr. Mercola. Here is an article in which he talks about oils and his recommendations for them. I was very glad to learn that I have been using the right oils for quite some time now. If you'd like to read the whole article, it is available here: http://articles.mercola.com/sites/articles/archive/2010/10/22/coconut-oil-and-saturated-fats-can-make-you-healthy.aspx.

Healing Your Environment

I considered myself a germaphobe in the past and I loved using products such as bleach, Comet, Ajax and others on a regular basis. However, in my childhood household, we didn't have too many of those Western products. When I got into the healthy chapter of my life, I discovered how important the products that we ingest are, and how they affect our bodies when they come into contact with our skin, the air we breathe and the environment in which we live. The Extension Toxicology Network (a source of science-based information on pesticides from top U.S. universities) states, "chemicals can be absorbed through the skin and into the bloodstream, causing toxic effects." That's why it's so important to only put on your skin what you would be willing to put in your body.

When I discovered this, I tried to take myself back to the chapter of my life where I used to watch my mom and grandmothers clean the house. I tried to remember what they were using as household cleaners every day, and the three cleaning ingredients that jumped out at me were baking soda, white vinegar and mustard seed powder. We used them to clean dishes, pots, pans, bathtubs—everything. When the baking soda alone was not enough, we sprayed vinegar on any surface for a fifteen- to thirty-minute soak; the grime would come off almost instantly. Below are a few more recommendations that could be used as **alternatives** to harsh **chemical agents** that pollute your internal and external environments.

Mustard

You might already know that the mustard seed is packed with minerals, such as calcium, magnesium, phosphorus and potassium, making it a healthy seasoning option for everyday consumption. There are studies that show that mustard seeds may help prevent colon cancer due to the presence of antioxidants. In addition to using it for cooking, mustard powder has both antibacterial and anti-inflammatory properties, making it a go-to for natural cleaning.

Odor remover: To remove odor from a jar or a container, sprinkle the mustard powder inside the container, add a little bit of warm water and shake it very well. The odor should be gone right away; if not, let it sit for a few minutes and rinse it out after that.

Greasy pans cleaner: Allow the frying pan to cool off. Sprinkle the surface of the pan with mustard powder. With a damp sponge, spread the formed paste on the entire surface in circular motion. Rinse with warm water. Repeat if the grease is not completely dissolved.

Detox and Other Practical Recipes

Apple Cider Vinegar

As I mentioned, growing up, my mother made her own apple cider vinegar and used it quite frequently in cooking. I didn't really know how wonderful a product apple cider vinegar was until I started doing some research. The reason I was joking earlier about how apple cider vinegar for me is like Windex in the movie "My Big Fat Greek Wedding", is that I truly utilize it every day. It's a miracle substance that should be present in every household. While there are many varieties on the market, only the raw, unfiltered and organic apple cider vinegar should be used. Otherwise, the healthy properties our bodies need will be diminished. I have been using apple cider vinegar to help treat a variety of health conditions I've struggled with over the years. While certain sources stipulate that apple cider vinegar doesn't contain enzymes that help with digestion, it has certainly impacted my gastrointestinal tract in a very positive way. One thing to always remember is to rinse your mouth with plain water after taking drinks with apple cider vinegar to prevent the teeth enamel disintegration. Here are a few practical uses that you could also put into practice.

Detox remedy with apple cider vinegar: Drink it upon rising (don't consume any drinks or food for at least twenty minutes after drinking it).

Ingredients

1. 1 tablespoon of apple cider vinegar
2. 1 tablespoon of raw, organic honey (ideally Manuka honey)
3. 1 cup warm water

Directions

Mix apple cider vinegar with water and honey and drink it twenty minutes before breakfast. It has detox effects on the liver.

Sore throat and cold remedy:

Ingredients

1. 4 tablespoons apple cider vinegar
2. 4 tablespoons warm water

Directions

Mix apple cider vinegar with water and gargle for at least fifteen to twenty seconds. Rinse your mouth with water. Repeat several times throughout the day.

Bug-repellant remedy: Fill a spray bottle with fifty percent apple cider vinegar and fifty percent water and spray your entire body before going outdoors. If you get bitten by a mosquito, spider or another bug, just spray the area as soon as you were bitten and let it dry. Don't be concerned that you could potentially smell like a salad dressing, as the apple cider vinegar scent diminishes very quickly.

Anti-burn and anti-fungal remedy: Apply full-strength apple cider vinegar on the burned area or the area that has been affected by fungus several times throughout the day until you see noticeable results.

Sore throat and cold remedy with mustard powder:
Due it its antimicrobial properties, mustard powder can be used to alleviate the symptoms of a sore throat.

Ingredients

1. 1 tablespoon of mustard powder
2. ½ cup warm water

Directions
Mix mustard powder with water and gargle for fifteen to twenty seconds a few times a day. In certain instances, to increase the antimicrobial properties, you can also add a teaspoon of baking soda.

Turmeric

I love Mediterranean cuisine. I often find myself savoring every last bite of their delicious chicken or rice entrées. But being the naturally curious person that I am, it had me wondering about the yellow color of those foods, only to find out later that the color was attributed to the mighty curcumin that is present in turmeric. Again, curious me, I started researching turmeric, just to ensure that it was not detrimental to my health. In the process, I was fascinated to learn that turmeric not only provides color and taste to food, but also possesses anti-inflammatory and antioxidant properties, and also has the ability to reduce swelling in your body. Turmeric is also very effective in reducing headaches naturally, unlike aspirin or ibuprofen, which damages your liver in the process.

Turmeric's antioxidant properties are capable of helping reduce or even, in some cases, prevent several types of cancers, such as prostate, breast, skin and colon cancer. Another amazing benefit is that frequent use of turmeric can lower the risk of developing diabetes and can improve liver function, which aids in removing toxins from your blood.

Here is one of the easy recipes that I incorporate into my practice quite frequently.

Detox remedy with turmeric:

<u>Ingredients</u>

1. Juice ½ lemon
2. 1 teaspoon turmeric
3. ½ teaspoon of raw, organic honey (ideally Manuka honey)
4. ¼ teaspoon black pepper

To boost the absorption of curcumin, black pepper, or some type of fat such as coconut oil, has to be added.

<u>Directions</u>

Add all of these ingredients to 1 cup of warm water (Not HOT, to preserve the vitamins in the lemon). Mix it well together and drink every morning on an empty stomach.

Headache relief remedy:

<u>Ingredients</u>

1. 2 teaspoons turmeric
2. ½ teaspoon black pepper

<u>Directions</u>

Add these ingredients to 1 cup of room temperature water. Mix it well together and drink it at the first signs on a headache. If the desired results are not achieved, make another drink 20-30 minutes later.

Toothpaste Recipe

Fluoride and other detrimental shelf-stabilizing ingredients are added to the store purchased toothpaste. The easiest way to avoid them, is simply to make your own toothpaste. Here is the one that I like making.

<u>Ingredients</u>

1. 5 teaspoons of calcium carbonate or Redmond bentonite clay or diatomaceous earth (your choice)
2. 2 teaspoons of baking soda
3. 5 teaspoons of coconut oil (to liquefy the coconut oil, add it to a small glass jar, close the lid and place the jar into a bowl filled with hot water until the coconut oil melts)
4. 12 drops of concern trace minerals
5. Mint, lemon, tea-tree or lavender essential oils

<u>Directions</u>

Mix all the ingredients in a glass bowl except the essential oil to ensure that all the ingredients are mixed properly. Use a teaspoon to scoop it out. Before brushing, add a drop of the essential oil to your toothbrush. While the color of the paste is not appetizing, this toothpaste is much healthier than the store-bought version.

Coffee Grounds

I love drinking coffee. While the debate about the benefits or risks of coffee is still not settled, I do drink a cup of organic coffee most mornings (but not until twenty minutes after my apple cider vinegar and water concoction) because of its antioxidant effects on the body. For that reason, I also save and use the coffee grounds, instead of disposing them or adding them to potted plants. I collect them and once a week I mix one fourth of a cup of coffee grounds with one fourth of a cup of baking soda and use it to scrub my entire body. The skin becomes smooth and clean of all impurities, and the coffee grounds also provide a slightly detoxifying effect on the body.

Cornmeal

I like to use cornmeal and baking soda to remove body odor instead of soap. Cornmeal is a type of corn flour and is more natural than soap. I mix one fourth of a cup of cornmeal with one fourth of a cup of baking soda and use it as a scrub.

Sour Cream

Got a sunburn? Apply sour cream on the affected area. While Aloe vera should be present in every household, as it is the easiest way to alleviate the pain of the excess exposure to the sun, it's good to have options, and sour cream might be readily available in your fridge.

Sauna

While living in Moldova, another activity that I enjoyed engaging in was going to the sauna. As summers are very hot in that part of the world, and winters extremely cold, saunas were something that I would start going to almost every Saturday from October through March. Up until recently, I thought the reason I loved it so much was because I was having a lot of fun with my friends. This certainly was a contributing factor, but later I discovered that sauna actually detoxifies our bodies. In the sauna, we would scrub our bodies with cornmeal instead of using soap. This left us feeling relaxed and filled with energy.

Epilogue

As you can see, my life has presented me with challenges but if there's anything that came out of that time, it is that I had the opportunity to experience enough for everyone. If by sharing my experiences I can help someone in the process, it was completely worth it. I've tried to make your transformation as easy as possible by doing the research for you so you don't have to agonize over the computer, wondering if the information you found is trustworthy or accurate. Especially with so much information to sift through, I know how difficult it can be to know where to start, which is why I wrote this book.

All of these tips and tricks have helped me out of the deepest corners of my mind, and I'm hoping that, if you follow this blueprint, you can apply it to your life and begin to experience positive results yourself. The ultimate goal is complete and utter peace from within. It starts with wanting to change your life for the better. By reading this book, you've already proved to yourself that you're willing to make the first step. Keep going. Don't forget to be kind to yourself and others, and write in your gratitude journal every day so that the cycle of joy, bliss and happiness is constant. You *will* notice a change in your life.

Thank you for reading *Old Country Wellness and Happiness Guide*. I'm grateful to have had the opportunity to share my story. **Welcome to the** new and beautiful you. **You are and look amazing! Be surrounded by love, peace, joy, happiness and gratitude.**

As I would like to continue supporting you in your journey, I have two free gifts for you:

1. ***Recipes Booklet*** filled with tasty recipes that you could incorporate into your daily cooking. Please email me at recipes@oldcountryhealth.com to receive your own copy.
2. ***Gratitude Journal*** filled with personal examples that will serve as a thought starter for your own journal. Please email me at gratitude@oldcountryhealth.com to receive your copy.

Results may vary. Information and statements made are for education purposes and are not intended to replace the advice of your doctor. This book does not dispense medical advice, prescribe or diagnose illness. The views and nutritional advice expressed by the author are not intended to be a substitute for conventional medical service. If you have a severe medical condition or health concern, see your physician.

Printed in the United States
By Bookmasters